GOOD

Young Butterfly

30 Days of Affirmation, Inspiration & Application

Self-Esteem Edition

Na'Kole Watson

Printed in the United States of America.

ISBN-13: 978-1979339025

ISBN-10: 1979339023

First Edition

Definitions used in this work were obtained from the following source:

Grove, Philip Babcock. "Webster's Third New International Dictionary of the English Language, Unabridged: a Merriam-Webster." Webster's Third New International Dictionary of the English Language, Unabridged: a Merriam-Webster, Merriam-Webster Inc, 2002, m-w.com.

Dedication

I would like to dedicate this book
to my Little One,
Miss KimberlyRuth Printess.
Thank you for being the best
little cousin in the world. Thank
you for always encouraging me
and keeping me motivated. I
love you so much! ♥

Dear Young Butterfly ♥

Thank you so much for taking the time to go through this book! It is my prayer that you will be encouraged, motivated and inspired as you complete each page! It's really simple: You start on Day One, and you keep going until you're done! Enjoy this journey. Make it memorable. Make it fun! I promise you that if you put something into this, you'll get something out of it! I look forward to hearing about your progress and success! If you ever need me, just email me at **nakole@nakolewatson.com**.
I'll email you back as soon as I can!

Be Lifted,

Na'Kole Watson

Day 1

Affirmation

Repeat these words as often
as you need to!

I have
CONFIDENCE
in myself.

Day 2

Journaling

Write a thoughtful and truthful journal entry about today's topic!

Name
three
things
you're
good
at.

Day 3

One Word

Take a moment to think about today's word and what it means!

vivacious

adjective

having much high-spirited energy and movement

Day 4

Action

We can't have words without actions! Enjoy today's activity, and feel free to write about it on the yellow Doodle Page!

Make a playlist of motivational music!

Doodle Page

Day 5

Journaling

Write a thoughtful and truthful journal entry about today's topic!

What do you like the most about yourself?

Day 6

One Word

Take a moment to think about today's word and what it means!

beatitude

noun

*a feeling or state
of well-being and
contentment*

Day 7

Action

We can't have words without actions! Enjoy today's activity, and feel free to write about it on the yellow Doodle Page!

Give out three compliments today!

Doodle Page

Day 8

Affirmation

Repeat these words as often
as you need to!

I am not better than anyone, and no one is better than me.

Day 9

Journaling

Write a thoughtful and
truthful journal entry about
today's topic!

What makes you unique?

Day 10

One Word

Take a moment to think about today's word and what it means!

confidence
noun

*great faith in
oneself or one's
abilities*

Day 11

Action

We can't have words without actions! Enjoy today's activity, and feel free to write about it on the yellow Doodle Page!

Look in the mirror and say three positive things to yourself!

Doodle Page

Day 12

Journaling

Write a thoughtful and truthful journal entry about today's topic!

Write about a time when you were proud of yourself.

Day 13

Affirmation

Repeat these words as often as you need to!

I am
intelligent.

Day 14

Journaling

Write a thoughtful and truthful journal entry about today's topic!

List three things you want to improve about yourself.

Day 15

Action

We can't have words without actions! Enjoy today's activity, and feel free to write about it on the yellow Doodle Page!

Take fifteen minutes and only think happy thoughts!

Doodle Page

Day 16

One Word

Take a moment to think about today's word and what it means!

extraordinary
adjective

being out of the ordinary

Day 17

Journaling

Write a thoughtful and truthful journal entry about today's topic!

Name
three
things
that are
special
about
you.

Day 18

Affirmation

Repeat these words as often
as you need to!

I AM
strong.

Day 19

One Word

Take a moment to think about today's word and what it means!

innovative

adjective

having the skill and imagination to create new things

Day 20

Journaling

Write a thoughtful and
truthful journal entry
about today's topic!

Write down ten words that describe you.

Day 21

Action

We can't have words without actions! Enjoy today's activity, and feel free to write about it on the yellow Doodle Page!

Do your favorite dance! If you don't have one, just dance! If you can't dance, dance anyway!

Doodle Page

Day 22

One Word

Take a moment to think about today's word and what it means!

jovial
adjective

indicative of or marked by high spirits or good humor

Day 23

Affirmation

Repeat these words as often
as you need to!

I am
POWERFUL.

Day 24

Journaling

Write a thoughtful and truthful journal entry about today's topic!

Write a happy letter to yourself.

Day 25

Affirmation

Repeat these words as
often as you need to!

I am beautiful.

Day 26

Journaling

Write a thoughtful and truthful journal entry about today's topic!

What is the greatest accomplishment you have ever made?

Day 27

Action

We can't have words without actions! Enjoy today's activity, and feel free to write about it on the yellow Doodle Page!

Do something special for yourself today.

Doodle Page

Day 28

One Word

Take a moment to think about today's word and what it means!

mindfulness
noun

a state of being aware

Day 29

Action

We can't have words without actions! Enjoy today's activity, and feel free to write about it on the yellow Doodle Page!

Tell yourself how AWESOME you are... because you are ABSOLUTELY AWESOME!

Doodle Page

Day 30

Affirmation

Repeat these words as often as you need to!

I am an **amazing** *individual.*

You did it!!!!!!!

You made it all the way to the end! I'm proud of you! Remember to visit http://NaKoleWatson.com to stay connected! Talk to you soon!

XOXO,
Na'Kole Watson

89669491R00044

Made in the USA
Columbia, SC
20 February 2018